WOMEN LIKE ME

KENYAN WOMEN SHARE THEIR STRENGTH,
WISDOM & LOVE

JULIE FAIRHURST

ROCK STAR PUBLISHING

Compiled by Julie Fairhurst

Paperback Edition: ISBN: 978-1-990639-32-6
Interior & Cover Design by STOKE Publishing

Publisher:
Rock Star Publishing British Columbia, Canada Email: julie@changeyourpath.ca

CONTENTS

"If you want to go fast, go alone. If you want to go far, go together."
~African Proverb~
(often attributed to the Akan people of Ghana)

COLLABORATIVE PUBLICATION

This is a collaborative publication, and you may notice variations in writing style from one piece to another. This is intentional, as it allows each writer to share their story in its authentic voice, preserving the uniqueness of their contribution.

We believe their raw and genuine perspectives bring a richness to this collection that polished writing alone cannot capture.

Each story reflects the individual journey and truth of the writer, which we honor and celebrate.

Some of these women are "first-time authors, not professional writers, but they have poured their hearts and experiences into these pages.

Every woman participating in the Women Like Me program shares a common purpose: "If my story can help even one person, then sharing it is genuinely worthwhile.

The authors of Women Like Me – Kenya speak many beautiful languages, but English is not their first. Pastor Pauline lovingly interprets their stories into English so their voices can be heard around the world. We do our best to preserve their original tone, rhythm, and heart, keeping their words as close to their truth as possible.

"Until the lion learns to write, every story will glorify the hunter."
~African Proverb~
(popular in Nigeria and Kenya)

WHY WOMEN LIKE ME MATTERS IN KENYA

In the heart of Kenya, 26 extraordinary women have come together to do something few in their communities thought possible: share their stories with the world.

These women are widows, mothers, survivors, and everyday warriors. Many live in poverty, often without steady income, access to reliable healthcare, or the means to send their children to school.

But what they do have is their voice, and Women Like Me is helping them use it.

Why? Because when women write, the world listens.

The Women Like Me Kenya Book Project doesn't just publish books. It amplifies voices, sparks global connection, and creates real, tangible change.

All publishing costs, including editing, formatting, cover design, and printing, are fully covered by Women Like Me. This means these women don't pay a cent to tell their truth. Instead, 100% of the proceeds from book sales are directly returned to these women, helping them provide for their families, pay school fees for their children, purchase medicine, and meet their daily needs.

This is not charity.

This is a partnership. Empowerment. Dignity. Legacy.

By writing their stories, these women become authors, recognized, respected, and take pride in their work. Many have never held a brand-new book in their hands, let alone one with their name in the table of contents, and their words in the pages. That moment, when they see and hold the book for the first time, is transformational. You can see the light in their eyes. It's not just a book, it's proof: My story matters. I matter.

These books bring more than awareness. They bring hope. They build bridges.

Readers from around the world begin to understand the challenges these women face, and the unimaginable strength it takes to endure, survive, and rise. This is awareness that moves people to act.

To care.

To support.

To buy the book and become part of something bigger.

Every time you purchase a copy of this book (or volumes one through four), you're not just reading a story. You're rewriting a new one.

You're helping a mother feed her children, keep her daughter or son in school, or pay for a life-saving trip to the doctor.

And for the women of Women Like Me Kenya, that means the world.

So, thank you.

Thank you for seeing them.

Thank you for helping them rise.

And thank you for being someone who believes that stories, especially true ones, can change everything.

Julie Fairhurst

Founder, Women Like Me

"Wisdom is like a baobab tree; no one individual can embrace it."
~Akan Proverb~
(Ghana)

A MESSAGE FROM PASTOR PAULINE ATWITA

Nehema Fountain Church – Western Kenya
Leader of Women Like Me – Kenya Chapter

Greetings in the name of Jesus Christ,

I am Pastor Pauline Atwita, a servant of God and a proud leader of the Women Like Me community in Western Kenya.

At Nehema Fountain Church, we are Christians who love to worship the Lord with joy, with music, with prayer, and with hearts full of faith. Every Sunday, we gather in our village to praise God and support one another as we grow together in spirit and purpose.

We are praying for something beautiful, a church building of our own.

A place where we can gather freely.

A place where widows, orphans, and families can come together for worship, healing, learning, and love.

We are preparing and blessing the land. We believe God will send what we need to build His house. We pray that Heaven opens its doors and pours out provision, so that the vision becomes a reality.

Our dream is to not only build a church, but a place of growth.

A place where our children can be safe and learn life skills.

Where they can be taught how to build, create, and dream.

Where they can make tambourines, chairs, crafts, and a future.

With our own building, we can host small fundraisers, offer support to struggling widows, care for orphaned children, and grow in the spirit together.

We are thankful for the global Women Like Me community. Your prayers and support make a real difference. Through the books we've written together, we are learning to share our stories, build our confidence, and provide food and school fees for those in need.

This is more than a writing project — it is a blessing from God.

But the need continues.

Some of our members are ill and cannot afford medicine.

Many of our orphans lack shoes and uniforms.

Some walk very far just to attend church.

Still, we believe. We believe in God's timing. We believe in community. And we believe that with your prayers, support, and the grace of God, we will rise.

Please pray for us. Please walk with us, not for riches, but for restoration, healing, and hope.

From our village to your heart,

We thank you.

We bless you.

And we stand in faith.

With love and gratitude,

Pastor Pauline Atwita

Nehema Fountain Church – Kenya

Leader, Women Like Me – Kenya Chapter

If you would like to donate to our Kenaya Chapter ladies, please contact Julie Fairhurst at julie@changeyourpath.ca

"The child who is not embraced by the village will
burn it down to feel its warmth."
~African Proverb~
(originates from East and West African oral traditions)

PART 1

KENYAN WOMEN SHARE THEIR STRENGTH, WISDOM & LOVE

1

JULIET OUTA

Do I Have Children?

"YES, I DO"

I'm a 37-year-old woman, a widow with four children.

I bring up my children in a way that they understand being orphans. I teach them patience and accept what life we live. There are ups and downs. They accept the day's income we get, and when we don't I've got a small, scaled business that helps me feed my orphan children.

As part of the business, I don't choose what work to do; I do any that comes ahead, i.e., washing other people's clothes and digging. For others, this is only to earn something for the day. This makes my children eat and be able to put clothes on.

For their education, I plant some vegetables and bananas and take to school for their school fees.

The little I get, the little I take to school as they continue learning.

When I miss taking the little I have to the school, I go to the school as a parent to defend my children, so that they may continue learning.

I am a woman who volunteers to share my strength so that my children can learn. I also teach them to know God and fear him, for he is the provider of everything in life, more so our lives.

The Lord will always protect.

The head of the Word of God makes them respect even the government and the world itself.

My children are also hard-working. This will make them have a colourful future.

My dear fellow women like me, there are difficulties and downs in life, especially in single-parent care! I must do it, even when it is so hard and different from bringing up on my own, but I thank God for the grace.

"He who learns, teaches."
~Ethiopian Proverb~

2

JESCA NIBAYI

What I think about marriage.

Praise God!

I thank God for my life, and I thank him because he blessed me with a good and handsome husband, and also blessed me with children. I thank him because he always protects my family.

My marriage always gives me power and praises the word of God, because without that, I can't be called a servant of God. My husband always tries, up and down, to ensure that our children are well-educated and have food and shelter.

A good marriage comes from God, and it is a must that you know first who God is so that you can advise other people. And it's good in my life as well. I try to teach my children the word of God because He's the only one who gives me.

I also appreciate my Pastor, Pauline, because she always tries to give us advice on how we can do well in our marriage and how we can protect our family. A good marriage also needs to have peace, faithfulness, and also love.

I understand my husband and also love him. Because he also advised me about the blood of Jesus. On respecting my body and my elders. I love my family because that's the work of God. My husband and I will always make sure we fulfill our goals to make our marriage happy and enjoyable.

In this world, it's good to get married and also have a family so that people can respect you; without that, you can be put in a bad group, which God can not be happy with you.

On my side, I thank God for that because I am well blessed with family.

"Even the best cooking pot will not produce food."
~African Proverb~
(from Sierra Leone; meaning that effort is required to create results)

3

CYNTHIA MAPESA

What do I do when I feel sad or lonely?

Loneliness is a state of being alone due to certain reasons or situations.

I am a 26-year-old Kenyan woman. I have a family of two kids, a boy and a girl, with one husband.

Life as an African woman is neither entirely good nor entirely bad, as it presents both challenges and difficult situations. At this time, life is good and times are bad.

On my own, I am a saved Christian.

When I feel lonely or sad, it can be due to marriage challenges or life. I usually go to my Pastor for guidance. Whenever I see her, I feel my problem revealed.

One advantage I have is that I live near her. Her teachings and guidance make me a happy woman. When she is not around, I find assistance from other women who are older than me in married life in our church.

Whenever situations are so tight that I cannot reach any of those, I usually find my nearest weapon, which is the bible. By reading God's word, I feel relieved because it teaches about many challenges and how to overcome them in our lives.

God's word and knowledge always make me happy. For now, what I can say is that more sadness is not in my life because we have books like 'Women Like Me'. I read it and I read the story of other Women Like Me in our book, and then I became very happy.

I want to say, sister Julie, with your vision of writing your books. You have healed my heart and my family

Be blessed, all Women Like Me

"Rain does not fall on one roof alone."
~Cameroonian Proverb~
(A reminder that hardship touches everyone.)

4

ELIZABETH CHISEKA

Some challenges I went through.

I am saved. I am a mother of five children, two of them are alive, and I thank God. I am 48 years old and have been married for 28 years.

There are many challenges that I am passing through in my lifestyle, e.g., school fees, providing food for my family, but in all, I succeed through the name of Christ in all the years that I have been married.

My husband is jobless, which has made me patient and want to have the voice of my God. Also, my husband's family has rejected me and my family, too. But in God, I cannot fear, because God is on my side.

To make it worse, I had an accident on my right leg, and this has even worsened my life. It is difficult for me to provide due to this situation.

When you read Philippians 4:13, it says that we can through Christ who strengthens us. This scripture always encourages me, whichever circumstances I pass through, I remain strong.

And God will keep me in all, but I want to thank Sis Julie for introducing this group of Women Like Me.

When I was alone at home, I thought I was the only one passing through this life. But when I got Women Like Me in Kenya from Pastor Pauline, my life changed because the stories of my friends in these books made me realize that I'm not the only person in this situation.

I thank this group.

Amen

"A single bracelet does not jingle."
~Congolese Proverb~
(Speaking to the power of unity.)

5

IRINE INDAKWA

How do you stay strong when life is difficult? It is healing!!!!

There are true difficulties in life, my dear fellows. In my life, I've faced many difficulties, for which I thank God for His total grace. The lord's grace has made me overcome the difficulties I face in life.

At times, I fail to understand how it all happens because in the past, the issue of poverty denied me a chance to go to school. It forced me to get married to a jobless man who was also an orphan. We continued with our lives until we started having children.

Today, I am a mother of six, though not easy.

Things turned upside down in my life, but the grace of God turned it back to its position. I was driven away from my family due to rumors from my neighbours that made my husband do away with me.

It was such a difficult time because the rumors were not true. God gave me some strength and I stood firm.

And what helps me is being part of the Women Like Me group; this group has surely helped me. It has more encouragement and teaches us how we can stay strong when things are not going well.

All women like me in Kenya and all over the world, God bless you all. Because it was very hard for me

These books of Women Like Me are good for those women who are struggling in their lives.

Try reading them and you will see it.

"Money can't talk, yet it can make lies look true."
~South African Proverb~

6

EMELDAH WANZALA

I am a Woman Like Me from Kenya.

I have so many things that I would like to share with other ladies like me.

I am a mother blessed with one husband and blessed with children. I thank God for that. In this world, there are so many challenges and lessons you can learn.

First thing, learn to look for God through deep prayers in order to overcome temptation in life.

Our homesteads, some are blessed, while others are still fighting.

In order to make their life better, never look at their lifestyles because in this world, all are not the same. In all, look for the lord because the word of the Lord said, "gold and money belong to him."

In spite of all challenges in life, like a lack of money, sickness, and no food. You have a husband, but he is not providing for the family.

Do not look behind, but instead look forward to what you are aiming for in life because you have to undergo challenges for you to be strengthened in the Lord.

Our dear Mothers, in this world we are blessed with children, so please make sure you take care of them. I may advise you to just look for God through prayer and fasting because God always hears and answers our prayers

"When there is no enemy within,
the enemies outside cannot hurt you."
~African Proverb~
(Widely used in Zimbabwe and across East Africa,)

7

EVELYNE MULLSTI

What advice would I give to other women going through hard times?

The first advice I will give to other women is that they need to join others because when you remain alone, you can have a day of stress.

If you want to live a long life, you need to share your story with women and share it with any person who can direct your advice well. Not everyone who knows how to advise, but you need to get a person who has good respect and can not talk to everyone about what you have shared with her.

And another thing I can advise is to join our group of Women Like Me because you will get stories in our books, and whatever situation you are going through, you will learn from other Women Like Me and their stories.

In the hard times, you need others.

You need to share what you are going through, and you will be ok. Share with your friends and women, and you will get rest.

You need to go to the church and learn the Word of God. The word of God can teach you, advise you, and encourage you on what you need to do next.

You need a church leader to discuss with you what Women Like Me can do as a leader to keep you blessed.

"When the roots are deep, there is no reason to fear the wind."
~African Proverb~
(Strength and foundation protect us from the storms of life.)

8

RUTH JUMA

What do I wish people knew about what I am doing in your life?

I want people in my life to know that I was an abandoned lady without any respect from anyone. A wife who had not understood that I was the mother of the family.

But I know people are looking at me, and I say I have changed in everything because I'm not drinking again. Alcohol has a way of teaching us from our lives. Our leader, Pauline, helps me. It wasn't busy; I was just home with nothing to do.

When I get, Pastor Pauline, a woman of God. She has taught me how to respect my husband and my family. I love my family, and I have joy with them.

I'm not sick again because I can cook the meal and have time to eat with my family

Indeed, 'Sure, Women Like Me' has changed my life. Because we are going to our meetings twice a month.

I am so very happy and log the lesson in our books, and I'm always very smart.

When people looked at me, they said Women Like Me is a good group where we have others, but they need to go to our group.

If you came to my home, it is very smart and clean, which is more about dialling in my life, so I am okay. I have a good lady and the stories in our books.

I'm full blessed to be in the group of Women Like Me in Kenya.

Amen

"Wisdom is not like money to be tied up and hidden."
~Akan Proverb~, Ghana
(Share your wisdom, it's meant to be passed on, not hoarded.)

9

RINA WANGA

My favorite memory in my childhood!

When I was young, I stayed with all my parents at home. When I was five years old, my father and mother took me to the nursery school.

When I recall standing eight, my education and I remained there because my parents were without school fees. But I remember at that time I was going to school without uniform shoes and without a pencil, but my book was small because my parents cut it out so I could use it for two subjects

When I was at home at the age of 15, I agreed to marriage because I had nothing to do.

My mom came and took me again. I think that she needed to take me back to school. But no, she takes me to go to the house first in Nairobi for work. But I stayed in Nairobi for three years and then I came back home to help my mom to ask jobs in the homes of people, but I thank God I get Pastor Pauline who has trained me to do many other things.

For now, I am in marriage, but I can take my children to school for now I have two children in high school. I can pay for school fees, I'm doing the work of a soldier.

And I am okay with the Women Like Me teachings from Julie and Pauline I am very happy and blessed.

"A bird does not change its feathers because the weather is bad."
~Nigerian Proverb~
(Be true to who you are, even in difficult times.)

10

JANE MAKOKKHA

What do I love about being a woman?

On my behalf, I love being called a mother and educating mothers. I am a mother with a family of six children and one husband.

At my residence, I like to be called mother with children since there are others who have not been blessed with children. I have some things I need to encourage them, like Women Like Me. I can say this is God's plan. But don't stay alone because you need someone to talk to.

If you visit the orphanage school, you can help children stay there. All women need to stay with people or with children; it's good to stay with them. Every woman is very happy when she stays well, without sickness and stress. I am very happy to stay without this.

Being a woman is a good thing for my family and church since a woman is the pillar of the family, despite challenges like my husband not providing for the family as a woman.

I must make sure that my family is well and with a lot of joy, like other children outside. However, I do my small work at home and plant my small meals like cassava, maize, and potatoes.

I'm very happy to be a mother who can provide for my family in this way.

As a woman, I live with my husband, and I love my family. I strive to make sure my family is okay with a lot of discipline, and being a woman.

Having a family and husband passing in all challenges and difficulties, and I love to be a Women Like Me.

"When the music changes, so does the dance."
~Hausa Proverb~, Nigeria
(Adaptability is wisdom; flow with life's rhythm.)

11

SWIZEX WESONGA

The small things that make a big difference in my life.

I come from a background and am the firstborn with seven children who lost their parents at the age of 15 years old. Being left in the hands of relatives, I married in the same year at the age of 15, to a Muslim man who treated me no better than a slave.

I went through hell in this marriage, and got depression, and was hospitalized every time with my kids. I suffered, and after 17 years, I was thrown out to die, but a man of God picked me up. I was born again and started life again as a Christian, but along the way, he died and left me again in his home, and his family started mistreating me.

I ran away with my kids to the streets. I went to approach and seek help, and I was given a small room. From there, I became a worshiper and a preacher as well, but my life changed significantly.

Due to a lack of shelter, job, and education for my kids, I have struggled to educate them. My first-born dropped out, and he is suffering from bipolar disorder at home. My second-born child pursued a career in graphic design without a job. My third-born, who is a girl, is 15 and is also pursuing fashion and modelling, with the help of friends.

I met a friend who helped me receive my first music, by the name Cricononi (meaning "in your hand"). I was delighted, and now I will be able to stay well because, through music, I will earn a living, and the money will help me. However, I have never sold a song. But technical ministry and singing make my life good.

It may seem like a small thing, but to me, it brings great joy.

Another thing is that he is a friend and talks to and counsels young men. It brings something different to my life. I love singing, worshiping, and counseling; it has made a big difference in my life.

Salvation is keeping me alive today. My advice is to work for God. I am a worshipper in this ministry, and it really makes a difference for all the rest.

I went through rejection when I was born again, which made me live a neglected life with humiliation, criticism, blackmail, and homelessness. I have a variety of interests, and working for God makes a significant impact on society.

I have lived in people's homes, cooking for them, though it was humiliating and a rejection. I learned how to cook good food, and also, I learned how to make clothes. As a result, I can make very nice garments; the only thing I lack is a good machine to do the work.

I have so many good things that make a big difference. I can also cancel a homeless person today because I have been on the streets for a long time until the woman of God, Pauline Atiwal, came to my rescue.

I can say she is my helper from God.

I worship in her church as a pastor and in many departments. And the small things really make a difference in my life, such as pure rice.

Thank you.

Shalom

"No matter how long the night, the day is sure to come."
~African Proverb~
(Hope endures, darkness never lasts forever.)

12

ANGELINE KWEYO

How do I stay hopeful when times are hard?

Hopeful is a state of being sure that you will attain whatever you need in your life in spite of challenges in your life.

I am a sixty-nine-year-old Kenyan woman. I am blessed with six children.

I have been a widow since my husband died. Life is not very easy due to ups and downs, challenges, and difficulties. I have to look after the family, both children and grandchildren.

This has made me very weak, and I am sickened now and then. Due to overworking, I have come up with health problems like chest pains, back pains, but in spite of all those, you have to make sure that your children are well both in feeding and education.

I have only one hope in life, and that is the word of God. This makes me make sure that I attend church service in order for me to hear the word of God, because it teaches me that God greeted me and he knows my life.

I want to appreciate the Women Like Me group in Kenya and its founder. Who are Pastor Pauline and Sister Julie? This group has made me strong because I'm very busy all the time.

We get encouragement from Pauline. She is the first person to tell me anything in my life. She is a good MUM. She has blessed us with meals and sometimes soaps, sugar. She has a heart of God. Women Like Me is a good group here in Kenya.

Thanks

"You learn how to cut down trees by cutting them down."
~Bantu Proverb~
(Experience is the best teacher, we grow by doing, not waiting.)

13

ANN KWEYU

The one talent I have that makes me special.

I'm very happy to be part of this group of women like me in Kenya, led by Pastor Pauline and Sister Julie. I have the talent of singing in the church, and I have the talent to encourage young mothers in the church. It makes me happy.

I like to sing gospel in the church. I was praying to earn money as an international singer, but it wasn't happening for now. I am many years old. It cannot happen again for now, I am 63 years old.

And for now, what I can do is farming because I come from a poor family, so they can not help me. My husband died, so my life is very hard. We are planting maize, and to get seeds, it's very hard with me because I don't have anyone to help me.

I have children, one girl and two boys. My children are drunks; they can not help me. Every time they are going to drink alcohol. So, I am like a person without children.

I would like to express my gratitude to Pastor Pauline, who blessed me with maize, soap, cooking oil, and sugar.

So, my talent in singing has died, but I still have hope that one day God will help my children to leave alcohol, and they will sing like me.

If we have a Women Like Me group in Kenya. We are receiving healing from Pauling, and now I'm very strong, and I believe I'm changed in everything.

Amen

"A single stick may smoke, but it will not burn."
~African Proverb~
(We are stronger together. Unity brings strength and lasting impact.)

14

BELDINE AOKO

The advice I would give to another woman going through hard times.

Hello Women Like Me, I would like to take this opportunity to thank our almighty God for all that we have achieved so far. It's his grace that some of us live today.

I have personally lived an unbelievable life to the extent that no one believes me. It's such a hard time, whereas I'm somehow disabled due to unfair conduct, and have had surgery for ten years now!

I'm a mother of three with a jobless husband. It forces me to struggle with how my family and I survive.

I find it easy because of the good connections with others, i.e., Women Like Me.

The Women Like Me strengthen, encourage, and keep me busy all the time, and their hard work makes me perceive a lot.

Despite the hardships in life, every dream becomes true whenever I come together with Women Like Me. They always make my dreams come true.

Therefore, I would urge you to join the Women Like Me group to make your hard time easier. They'll share and help change your attitudes to a better future.

You won't see the hardness any longer. As long as you agree to walk together, share, and work hard with them. Many times, most of the Women Like Me live like widows today, even though they have their unsupportive husbands with them.

It is found that most of the men only marry to develop children in their wives' wombs; after that, their work is over.

They don't support, they don't respond, nor do they care about their families. Today, the husbands will see their wives change lives go ahead without their support, just because of the Women Like Me who decided to change their lives.

It is healing, it is time; there are women who have experienced life and decided to make it change.

My dear fellow women, let's join the group and change lives.

"Even the best dancer on the stage must retire sometime."
~African Proverb~
(Stay humble. No one holds the spotlight forever.)

15

AGNESS AMUKURU

The advice I would give the young ones.

I am a mother who can advise the young ones.

1. Young ones, what can I tell them fast is to respect their parents and to stay humble to the country, because in the world they will meet different people.
2. Our young people need to go to school and remain strong in their education because, without going to school, they will not have a good life. Education is the key to everything.
3. Do not allow an alala marriage to be good because you are too young to serve in their life. Life is very hard if you are not being educated, so just remain humble so you can finish your education or school.
4. Life sex doesn't allow it in you, life, we have sickness and HIV. We have children whose parents got pregnant when they had HIV. And when you get there, they cannot tell you that they are sick. When you sleep with them, you will get diseases, so young ones, be very careful.

5. Respect the leadership in your village because they will say you do have good career and they can get something like good job they cannot tell you because of your connection.
6. Go to the church every Sunday. We have a lot to learn there.

GOD BLESS ALL YOUTH

"No matter how hot your anger is, it cannot cook yam."
~Nigerian Proverb~
(Anger alone achieves nothing. Patience and action are more powerful.)

16

VERONICA MUIAYI

The lessons I learned from my mum and grand mum.

I learned many things from my mum and grand mum.

My mum was a person who had a heart because my father was a bad person. He was beating mum every day, but you can not get mum to tell you about that story, but you will see my mum, she has no joy.

My father was not providing anything to us, so every morning my mum would wake up, and Alia and she would go to the lands of people to ask for a job. When she gets the job, she will come with maize flour and green vegetables, and she will cook and give to us like family with our father.

I learned from my mum; she was very hardworking.

Another time, she will go ask for a job to buy us clothes and soap. If it were tea we were drinking, and green tea without sugar, that was okay, but our health was good and strong.

My Mum was a strong woman who was disciplined in the village and with us as a family. Our mum teaches us that if you cannot get a job, be a man. You need to learn how to stand and feed your family.

How she'd been doing. There is not a day I have seen my father providing for our family; I see only a mum who has been doing everything. My mum has been doing the job at Caden until she builds the house.

Which is not easy for another woman. I lean a lot on my mum. She has taught me how to cook, how to wash my clothes, how to cope with harsh people, and how my children can attend school without my husband's support.

I can go to school and ask any teacher who has Caden. I can go digging for her and give her some money to pay my children's school fees.

This is the life I'm living today.

Thank you, all Hallelujah,

"The eagle does not hunt flies."
~African Proverb~
(Greatness doesn't waste time on petty things. Stay focused on your purpose.)

17

JANE AMABIA

How I support my family.

My name is Jane Amabia. I come from Emukoa. I am blessed with a husband and also blessed with children.

I have already tried to fulfill my family's needs by supporting them. I ensure they receive good shelter and also educate them. God blessed me with a small business of selling mangoes with oranges.

That place makes me to have faith so that God me them so it's a must they "what to do" I passed through many challenges which by I didn't know what to do but God tried to guide me so that my children to be off.

Without God, I wouldn't be the way I am, because my small business always provides me with shelter, school fees, and clothes for my children. I thank God because I always praise His name, for He has changed my life.

What I always get per day is what I'm used to. In the West, we often rely on potatoes, cassava, and other staples, so we don't have problems with food shortages. But we struggle to get what we can do.

Also, my husband tried his best to ensure our family's well-being by giving us a small amount, which allowed us to buy food and pay school fees. But in my family, when they lack food and shelter, they don't have peace, but if you know the word of God.

God always gives you whatever you need in your life.

My family is so happy because we always praise the name of God, and we get everything we lack.

"A mother is gold; a father is a mirror."
~Ganda Proverb~ (Uganda)
(A mother is precious and foundational, while a father reflects identity.)

18

PHEIESIA ABUKO

This is what I love about being a woman.

I am 46 years old. I have nine children. I'm very happy to be a woman and mother of my children.

I'm very happy to be somebody's woman. I am in a marriage for many years. I have learned a great deal from the women in my life, including my marriage.

We have many women who are not in a marriage, but they are still women I would speak with. They are women like others, they are special like others, so it's good to be a Woman Like Me.

I am a woman who loves to be in my home. I am doing everything because I need to be a woman who can stand as the mother of my family.

I am very busy with my work at home. I plant Caden, I plant vegetables, Maize, and beans for my family to eat, and I can sell the rest for school uniforms and buy shoes for my children.

I'm not looking for my husband because my husband is a very bad person in our lives. He can not care for the children. My husband is like a child who will ask me what he can eat, what soap he can use, and even what he can use in our house.

In my home, I love to be a woman because God has helped me to be strong.

Women Like Me, and to join women's groups that are older than me.

I'm very happy to have women who were more knowledgeable, Sis. Pauline and Sis. Julie. I'm very happy to be with Women Like Me and other ladies.

For now, I am very happy in my heart

Thanks

"A child who does not cry will die on his mother's back."
~Kenyan Proverb~
(If you don't speak your needs, even those who love you may not know to help.)

19

JOSPHINE OKUMU

How do I celebrate special moments in my life?

My name is Josphine Aking Owumo. I am married and I am blessed with six children.

My life sometimes becomes hard, but I always thank God for it. But I always celebrate a special moment in my life by doing the work of God. I appreciate God because he loves my life and family, and also gives me the power to praise his word.

My family and I always sit together and start teaching each other about God's work. In our family, we always love that God is good in everything you pass through. So, in special moments we need to be together and now what God is doing in our lives.

However, on my side, I have faith because everything is going well. But I always think of Philippians 4:13 and remember what God does in my life.

It's better to know the word of God in our lives because he changes our situation. We live in Christ, we celebrate his work, and we love him because he's the only one in our lives.

Let us appreciate everything and advise others about the word of God in life.

And to join together as one family with God and Women Like Me in the world. If you join Women Like Me, you will be happy and always be blessed.

"A mother cannot give birth to a child and refuse to suckle it."
~Nigerian Proverb~
(A true mother embraces both the birth and the responsibility of love.)

20

MAGRET OTUBULA

What makes me happy in my daily life?

I am Margret Otubula. I am 71 years old. God blessed me with 12 children, three died, and nine are alive.

I'm now a Women Like Me through practising the word of God.

What makes me happy in my daily life is how my parents took care of me. Though, having respect for older people. And also, how my life was when I was young. My parents tried their best to take good care of us, and they taught us about the word of God. As, we continued to grow and also attend services in the church, and to pray, every moment.

And, the good care of my parents led me to get a husband who is always in a position in our lives, and I appreciate what happened. But she later died and left me with all the children. I tried my best to fulfill their goals, which include getting food and education.

Now, I always advise the younger ones to cherish their marriage and family. To take care of their husband so that they can enjoy their life well.

The main focus in our daily life is to know the word of God and also serve him daily. Love your life, and God will also change the situations we pass through.

Another thing that makes me really happy is participating in Women Like Me in Kenya.

I teach them and encourage them, and we read our books, 'Women Like Me,' and enjoy them; this always makes me very happy.

Amen

"He who thinks he is leading and has no one
following him is only taking a walk."
∼Malawian Proverb∼
(True leadership is measured by impact, not position.)

21

LILIAN MUKONYI

What makes me happy in my daily life?

I am a married woman blessed with four beautiful girls named Sophy, Aggy, Neema, and Faith.

I live in a small village named Emikow, located in Kakamega County, in the western part of Kenya.

I am happy to be one of the Kenyan Women Like Me. The group has changed my lifestyle in the community. I can even help other mothers learn how to raise their families and be good mothers.

When I remember, some years ago. I passed through hardship, I could not even support my family. We had even quarrels with my husband, but when this group was introduced to us by a woman of God, Julie Fairhurst.

I am growing gradually stronger day by day. I always sit under the woman teaching to make a good wife and a good mother to others.

Most of all, I serve my God. Preaching his gospel to others. This has made and changed my daily life both spiritually and physically. My beloved husband always learns from me. I am actually a good leader to read to other nations. These are the fruits that I am getting for Women Like Me, Strong Women in Kenya.

Lastly, I salute Mama Julie for taking us a step forward. In Kenya, as strong women, we shall not move in poverty again, or be cursed.

This has made my live a happy life daily

God Bless

"Wisdom is like fire. People take it from others."
∼Hema Proverb∼ (DR Congo)
(Wisdom spreads through connection; we learn by sharing.)

22

PAULINE ATITWA AWMO

Sometimes I feel very tired.

When I fear I will die with something that was happening in my life or my family. I feel bad on my side, but I didn't come to tell anyone because I'm afraid to tell anyone.

But for now, when I feel bad, I just encourage my heart, and if it becomes very hard, I share my thoughts with my group in Kenya, which is Women Like Me.

But before I tell them, I ask myself how I can handle this, because if someone is tired, they cannot do anything good. Like me, I pray for it and then read the book Women Like Me because, for now, these books are like medication in my life.

When I read this book, I get what I can do. Sometimes you get tired. When you are feeding all your family, and you are a woman, and you have a husband. You get so tired, and it's not good. But you will not show the children, but your body will show them. Then you tell them that you are on a diet, because you will be weak.

When I feel tired of people who like to talk a lot, I separate myself to avoid temptation. So I don't like that I fear going where they are.

In Kenya, sometimes women are tired of doing everything, and we have a man who cannot help us or assist the children in school. So many women are struggling to make sure the family is doing well.

All women in the world, make sure your family is doing well. Just be hardworking in everything you do. Don't worry about what is happening in your life. Just be strong, don't be tired.

I love you all, Women Like Me.

I'm a leader of Women Like Me in Western Kenya. We are Christian who loves to worship God.

We come together in Women Like Me. We need to have a village church in our communities so we can hold small fundraisers. We are blessing the land for the actor to build our church where we can meet to worship our heavenly father. Who knows everything that we need? So we are in prayer for what we need. So we are in prayer that my true lord will open the doors of heaven to let us get our church.

Women Like Me, all over the world, we need your prayers and support.

We have our children, Women Like Me. If we open our church, and we can build another house there, we can take our children like you, and we can look for someone who knows how to make the future; they can teach them how to make things like tambourines, chairs, and coupons.

So, we need your prayers and support.

God Bless All

Amen

"Two ants do not fail to pull one grasshopper."
~Tanzanian Proverb~
(Working together, even the smallest can achieve the impossible.)

23

PATRICA FAITH

The one thing I want to teach my children for the future generation.

I need to teach them to love God. And to be with their parents and to receive the teaching from them.

They need to be in school so that they can avoid becoming like their parents, who have not saved in their lives because they are not educated.

They need to respect their parents, as well as the leadership that surrounds them. If they are a baby girl, do not enter into early marriage because their life will be very like their parents.

They need to work hard in everything. If God opens a way for the job, they need to be very hard working, and love everything they do.

These children need to love the word of God in their lives and go to, church every Sunday because it is not easy to get children to love God; they are robbers, but many are robbers because they do not respect their parents, pastors, and adult people.

If it is well, children will give greetings to everybody, so they can teach themselves to love one another and love themselves. They need to be humble to everyone.

Thank you so much, SIS Julie, for reaching out to Women Like Me.

God bless our team and all they offer to the world

"Rain beats the leopard's skin, but it does not wash out the spots."
~Ashanti Proverb~ (Ghana)
(Nature reveals, but does not change one's true character.)

24

ROSE JUMA

If I could change one thing in the world for women, this is what it would be.

If I could change one thing in the world for women, I believe all women in the world are managers, and they need to know that. Because if you visit the house without women, it's very different and sad.

It's not easy to get the house visited because the women are not in the house.

Women around the world, we have a lot to do so we can care for our families. Let us all know that we need to be strong and courageous, because if a woman is not strong in everything, her household will not be respectful to its neighbours or others.

We women can change to see that we are not weak.

We need to know that we can do everything that a man can do. We can give advice. You can change your life from 0 to 10. You will be a good woman.

Women don't always stay in the rear when things are not good with you. You are showing the world you are weak. Show the world that when it comes, you will overcome anything.

Good women have a vision of what they plan to do in their lives so that their lives may come easily. If you have children and you don't have someone to help you. Pray and find the way to solve your problems.

Change your life as you will. Speak loudly and fear not, and you will be well in your life.

God bless SIS Julie, Pastor Pauline, and the group of Women Like Me.

"Knowledge is like a garden: if it is not cultivated,
it cannot be harvested."
~Guinean Proverb~
(Insight without action bears no fruit.)

25

ROSE NYAROSTO

How do I show kindness to others?

I'm showing people that I love them, and I need them, and they need me.

Like women in the world and my friends, I can't stop showing kindness to others. I believe God is with me and my family, but my husband is letting me down because he remains drunk.

However, I thank God for all that I am sharing with people in my village and country. Join this group of Women Like Me, and you will not be in sad mode. This book, Women Like Me, has a lot more to teach us.

I have reason to show kindness to help them.

If I get a small thing, I help our people, such as teaching them how to cook meals, and how they can stay Godly in their lives. And how can they love one another in their life?

I'm telling them not to listen to those who are not good in their life— they need to serve with others.

I'm learning more from women of God, who is Pastor Pauline. Who is showing kindness to many people?

If she gets a small thing, she gives it out to us and our family. Another time, she bought books and a uniform for our children, so I am learning more from her

I love women like me in my country.

God bless all

"A large chair does not make a king."
~African Proverb~
(Titles don't define greatness, action and character do.)

26

UNICE NERIMA

What is my favourite memory from my childhood?

When I was young, I used to play with balls and play with the children from our neighbors' homes near ours. I was going to church with my mum when I was five years old. I don't like to go to school because many children beat me there. I was afraid to go to school.

Another time, my mum could buy things like a flat cake so that I could be happy to go to school, but when you get big children, they will come and take it all, my school bag. Our teachers can't say anything, so I refused to go back to school.

I want to give my thanks to my parents who have made me love school and finish school.

Now I know how to write anything that I need to write on my own. What I was thinking was that I wanted to be a nurse when I was young, but my dream has not come true because I didn't have the school fees. My parents were very poor. I want to continue with my education, but all is good.

I want to say that I think I will not learn again, but for now, I have a great teacher, who is Pastor Pauline.

For now, I'm learning what life has to offer and what I can do in my life. We are writing our books, and I'm very happy with what we are doing to come together as Women Like Me.

Thank you, our Founder, SIS Julie

"A leader who does not take advice is not a leader."
~Ghanaian Proverb~
(Wisdom listens. Ego silences.)

27

MONICA KHAYAS

A small thing that makes a big difference in my life.

A small thing that makes a big difference in my life is this group of women, like those in Western Kenya.

When I heard about this group, I was not ready to join it because there are many groups here in Kenya, but it wasn't a good fit for me. I have never entered any group because they cannot teach us how to stay with other things; it is not good.

But this group of Women Like Me has made a big difference in my life and my family.

For now, when something happened to me, the first person to come and be near me was Pastor Pauline, and this group. If they have money in the group, my problem will finish like that. So this group makes a difference in my life.

My children are going to school. Pauline tells us that it is a must for children to go to school.

Another time, we bet on books, and she blessed us with maize, soap, and cooking oil.

So, I have a big difference in my life. I'm very happy with Women Like Me in Western Kenya.

Amen

"You cannot build a house for last year's summer."
~Yoruba Proverb~ (Nigeria)
(Live in the present. You can't build your future based on the past.)

28

IMANI ORPHAN CARE FOUNDATION

THE DREAM THAT WOULDN'T LET GO
FOUNDER: KIM LEE

Introduction by Julie Fairhurst
Founder, Women Like Me

Some stories stay with you.

Others change you.

This one does both.

The story of Imani Orphan Care Foundation is not just about charity; it's about divine purpose, unshakable faith, and one woman's refusal to ignore the tug on her heart.

When I first met Kim Lee, she spoke about how her deepest sorrow became a source of hope for hundreds of children in Kenya. I knew this story belonged in our book. Not only because of what she's built, but because of *why* she built it.

Imani, which means *faith* in Swahili, is not just a name. It is the spirit that breathes through every child who has been fed, clothed, educated, and loved through this mission. It is the echo of a mother's love, one that reaches across oceans to answer the cries of children who were once forgotten.

This is a story about showing up.

About holding on.

About believing that love can rise out of loss and that one woman's "yes" to God can change the world, one child at a time.

I'm honored to share Kim's journey in these pages, and I hope as you read, you'll feel what I felt - that *this is what faith in action looks like.*

The Dream That Wouldn't Let Go

In the quiet of her Canadian home in Abbotsford, BC, a profound sorrow sparked an extraordinary mission. Kim Lee and her husband, Geoff, had endured the deepest loss imaginable: their daughter, Kennedy Faith, was stillborn in December 2006.

But from that heartbreak rose something beautiful — Imani.

In Swahili, Imani means faith. Faith that love can transcend grief, and that hope can chase away despair.

Before she ever set foot in Africa, Kim felt the tug of destiny.

Night after night, she dreamt of children reaching out to her, a silent SOS she couldn't ignore. The message was clear: Go. Listen. Love. Those dreams didn't stop until she did precisely that.

In June 2010, Kim and Geoff travelled to Kenya. She visited Mombasa, a bustling coastal city, and nearby villages, where she met children living without access to food, clean water, or even shoes on their feet. Though she felt God's hand guiding her, nothing truly prepared her for the scale of need she saw.

When Kim returned to Canada the following month, she knew this wasn't just a trip. It was a divine assignment. Her heart was now tied to the children of Kenya, and her next chapter was crystal clear.

From that moment, **Imani Orphan Care Foundation** was born. A Canadian charity rooted in faith, built on compassion, and committed to rewriting the stories of Kenya's orphaned and vulnerable children.

From Grief to Grace: A Movement Grows

Kim Lee didn't step into this mission with ease or a ready-made roadmap. She walked into it with faith and found herself immediately facing walls of red tape, cultural challenges, and a daunting financial hurdle.

Starting Imani Orphan Care Foundation wasn't a gentle beginning. It was an uphill climb through bureaucratic complexity, with the Kenyan government's requirements stretching long and winding. The funding needed for land, construction, and daily care of the children towered higher than she could have imagined.

But Kim didn't stop.

She didn't turn away.

She leaned *in*, heart-first, faith-forward.

There were days when it felt impossible. Times when the resources didn't match the need. But through every obstacle, Kim clung tightly to the vision and to God's promise that He wouldn't lead her to something He wouldn't also lead her *through*.

The money didn't simply show up at the doorstep. It was *worked for*. Fought for. Prayed over. Fundraising wasn't just an event; it became Kim's way of life.

She poured her energy into organizing initiatives like the **"Marathon of Hope" hockey tournament**. She rallied her hometown of Abbotsford, British Columbia, to believe in a mission happening thousands of miles away.

She spoke.

She shared.

She asked.

She prayed.

She said, "Yes", again and again, even when everything inside her wanted to rest.

Building homes for orphaned children in Kenya wasn't a feel-good project for Kim. It was a full-time calling that required 24/7 devotion. There were no off days, no guaranteed paycheques, and no backup plan.

Just one woman's promise to show up — *every single day* — so that children could be fed, clothed, educated, and loved.

And through that grit, that faith-fueled hustle, miracles began to unfold.

Land was bought.

Homes were built.

Children who once had no one now had everything they needed to thrive.

Because Kim said, "Yes", and then repeated it the next day. Because she believed that if she kept showing up, so would the blessings.

And what began as a response to personal sorrow has become something extraordinary, a *Home of Love* that wraps its arms around hundreds of children who once had nowhere to turn.

What started with tears of grief has bloomed into a life-giving sanctuary where laughter now echoes through hallways built on faith and relentless love.

Today, Imani Orphan Care Foundation supports over 250 children, not just with the basics, but with the fullness of what every child deserves:

- Nutritious meals served with care
- Clean water that sustains life
- Medical attention that brings healing
- Education that opens doors to a brighter future
- Spiritual guidance that anchors the soul
- Emotional support that says, "You are not alone."

But beyond the physical, Imani offers something even deeper: a sense of worth.

Here, children are not statistics. They are not problems to be solved or needs to be managed. They are cherished. They are celebrated. They are seen.

Each child is reminded daily that they are valuable, wanted, and deeply loved, not just by the caregivers around them, but by a global family that believes in their future.

In a world that often turns away from the most vulnerable, Imani stands as a radiant declaration:

You are not forgotten. You are not forsaken. You belong.

This is more than a home. This is a movement of love. A faith-fueled mission where brokenness is met with healing, and despair is answered with divine hope.

Because when one woman said, "Yes" to turning her pain into purpose, the ripple reached across oceans and continues to transform lives every single day.

About Imani Orphan Care

At Imani Orphan Care, our mission is to raise a new generation of Kenyan leaders who are bold, educated, and full of integrity. We believe that when children are given not just care, but opportunity, they can rise above their circumstances and become changemakers in their communities.

Through access to quality education, practical life skills, spiritual guidance, and unwavering love, we empower every child to grow into a responsible, compassionate, and purpose-driven citizen of Kenya.

We're not just meeting today's needs... we're building tomorrow's leaders.

Where We Work: Kenya, East Africa

Imani Orphan Care operates in the heart of Kenya, East Africa, a nation rich in culture, beauty, and resilience. But behind the vibrant landscapes lies a heartbreaking reality: over three million children are orphaned, many abandoned, vulnerable, or left without support due to poverty, disease, and crisis.

Nearly 47% of these children have lost their parents to HIV and AIDS, and countless others face hardship from hunger, unsafe living conditions, and lack of access to education or healthcare.

These children are not just numbers; they are sons and daughters, dreamers and survivors, waiting for someone to believe in them.

At Imani, we step into that gap, offering love where there was loss, stability where there was struggle, and hope where there once was heartbreak.

Changing the World — One Child at a Time

Imani Orphan Care is a registered Canadian charity, a recognized NGO in Kenya, and proudly holds 501(c)(3) status in the United States.

But more than a list of credentials, Imani is a promise. A promise to love, protect, and uplift children who come from the most desperate and heartbreaking circumstances.

We care for children who have been orphaned, abandoned, or rescued from unsafe environments, and we provide them with more than just shelter. We offer a safe, faith-filled home where they are nurtured, seen, and deeply loved.

Through God-centered guidance, a strong education, and life-enriching practical skills, we help each child break the cycle of poverty and step boldly into a future filled with hope.

Our mission is clear:

To raise up the next generation of Kenyan leaders, young people who pursue excellence, walk with integrity, and become responsible, purpose-driven citizens ready to transform their communities.

At Imani, we believe real change doesn't come from quick fixes! It comes from equipping children with the tools, knowledge, and love they need to thrive for a lifetime. It's a sustainable, soul-rooted approach that changes the trajectory of entire lives.

Be Part of the Change

You can be the reason a child survives and thrives.

By becoming an Imani Child Sponsor, you offer more than support. You give the gift of life, education, and a sense of belonging. You turn despair into dignity. Fear into faith. Poverty into possibility.

Sponsor a child today. Our kids are counting on you, and the world needs what they're becoming.

Visit www.imaniorphancare.com to learn more and become a sponsor.

"The child who is not taught by its mother
will be taught by the world."
~African Proverb~
(If we don't raise our children with love and values, the world will do
it without mercy.)

29

THE KENYAN BOOK SERIES

VOLUME ONE

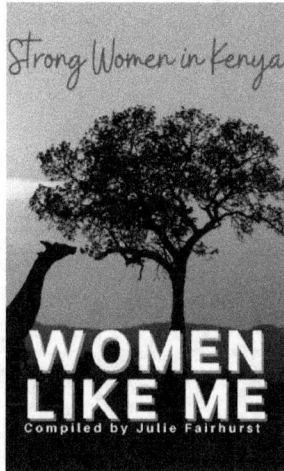

Women Like Me: Strong Women in Kenya

21 women. 21 voices. 21 reasons to believe in the power of story-telling.

In this groundbreaking first volume, 21 women from Kenya, many widowed, impoverished, and living without access to basic necessities, share their raw, real-life experiences.

These women had never imagined becoming published authors. But with courage and the support of the Women Like Me movement, they found their voices.

Proceeds are distributed directly to the authors to help cover the costs of food, medical care, and education.

(every penny) The publishing costs of the Kenya books were fully covered by Women Like Me.

This book is not just a collection of stories. It's a declaration:

We are here. We matter. And we are rising.

VOLUME TWO

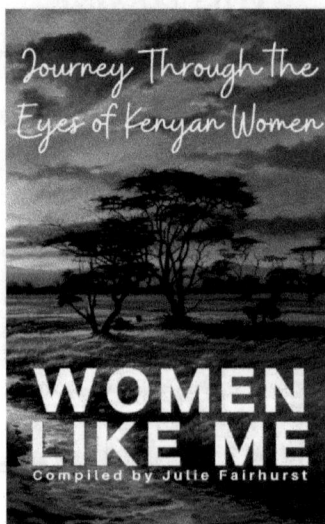

Women Like Me: Through the Eyes of Kenyan Women

Their pain is real. So is their power.

Volume Two welcomes 24 voices: mothers, daughters, widows, and survivors.

These women write with clarity and honesty about what it means to live through loss, poverty, illness, and injustice, while still holding onto hope. Through their eyes, we see the reality of rural and urban life in Kenya.

These stories are not polished fairytales. They're beautifully imperfect, fiercely human, and deeply moving.

Proceeds go directly to the women who wrote them.

Women Like Me covers all publishing costs to ensure their stories are told and their dignity preserved.

Every book bought is a bridge, from one woman's pain to another's possibility.

VOLUME THREE

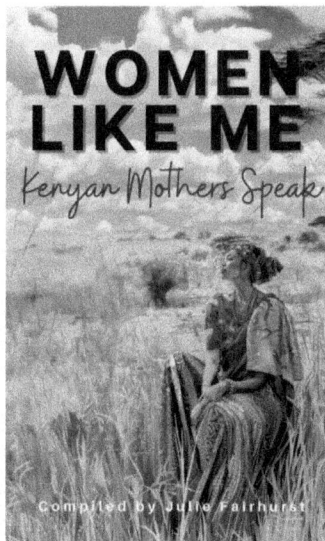

Kenyan Mothers Speak

The quiet heroes of Kenya finally speak. And the world is listening. This volume delves deeply into the hearts of mothers, women who raise children amidst overwhelming odds.

From struggling to put food on the table to navigating the loss of a partner or child, these women write not just as victims of circumstance but as warriors of love. Their stories will challenge your heart, open your eyes, and remind you of the strength that grows in silence. As with every *Women Like Me – Kenya* book, **100% of the profits go directly to the authors.**

This book is their voice, their victory, and their opportunity to rise. This book honors them. When you read it, so do you.

"Rats don't dance in the cat's door without a plan."
~African Proverb~
(Even the boldest have their reasons; every move has intention.)

PART 2

WOMEN LIKE ME PROGRAM

30

THE WOMEN LIKE ME COMMUNITY

A PLACE TO BELONG, A SPACE TO WRITE, A MOVEMENT TO INSPIRE

If you're not already part of the Women Like Me Community, I invite you to step into a space where women come together to uplift, empower, and share their voices. This is more than just a social network; it's a writing community filled with women who have stories to tell, wisdom to share, and dreams to bring to life.

Here, you'll find connection, encouragement, and inspiration from like-minded women who understand the journey of life, the power of words, and the importance of lifting each other.

Whether you're a seasoned writer, a first-time author, or someone who wants to share your truth, this is a place where your words matter.

Throughout the year, we collaborate on Women Like Me Community books, like the one you are reading now. Every woman in our community is invited to contribute, and there's no cost to participate, just a willingness to share your story and inspire others.

If you've ever dreamed of becoming a published author, this is your chance to take that first step in a supportive and welcoming environment.

More than just a writing group, the Women Like Me Community is a movement. Whether you're a working professional, an entrepreneur, or a stay-at-home mom, you'll find personal tools, role models, and friendships that will help you grow, not just as a writer, but as a woman embracing her full potential.

If you've been searching for a place where you can be seen, heard, and valued, this is it.

Your story matters. Your voice matters. You matter.

Please don't wait, join us today and start writing the next chapter of your life!

Our group is located on Facebook...

Write Like a Woman – Empowered by Women Like Me

https://www.facebook.com/groups/879482909307802

If there is no enemy within, the enemy outside can do no harm."
~African Proverb~
(Inner peace and self-belief are your strongest defenses.)

31

THE BOOK SERIES

Everyone has a story. And oftentimes, those stories can be powerful things that help us learn and grow.

But for some people, their stories can be a source of pain. They may feel like they can't escape their past or that their story is holding them back from living their best lives.

If you're one of those people, know that you're not alone. And more importantly, know that there is hope. There are ways to turn your personal story into something positive and to find healing from the past.

One way is to share your story with others. This can be incredibly cathartic, and it can also help others who have been through similar experiences. You process your feelings and work through any trauma you may be carrying around.

And finally, don't forget that your story doesn't define you.

- You are more than your history.
- You are more than your pain.

- You are more than your mistakes.
- You are more than your story.
- You are strong, you are brave, and you are enough.

So don't let your story hold you back.

Writing about your past can be very beneficial, both emotionally and psychologically. You can increase your feelings of well-being and even improve your physical health. When you write about your past experiences, you relive them in your mind. This can help you to process difficult or traumatic events, and it can also provide you with some closure.

Additionally, writing about your past can help you better understand yourself and work through any unresolved issues. It can also allow you to see yourself in a new light, which can be both healing and empowering.

In addition to helping you emotionally, writing about your past can also be beneficial physically.

Studies have shown that expressive writing can help to reduce stress, anxiety, and depression. It can also help to improve your immune system function and promote a sense of calm. So, if you're feeling stressed or overwhelmed, consider picking up a pen and starting to write.

We only have one shot at this life, and it's our only shot. There are no do-overs. There are no second chances. So, we better make the most of it.

We only have this moment right here, right now, and it's the only moment that matters.

We are only given so much time on this planet and must spend it wisely.

We only have so much energy and want to spend it on things that bring us joy.

We only have so much love and want to give it to people who appreciate it.

If you're a woman with life experiences, the world wants to hear from you. Visit my website at www.juliefairhurst.com and get in touch. The world will be waiting.

A story is powerful. It can draw you in, take you on a journey, and leave you with lasting impressions. That's why I love listening to other people's stories.

Everyone has a story, and I'm always eager to hear a new one.

I want to hear from you. You can reach me by visiting my website and letting me know you're ready to tell your story. The world is waiting to hear what you have to say.

Get in touch today!

Women Like Me Stories www.juliefairhurst.com there you'll find the Author Form to fill out and get started!

"When the roots are deep, the tree does not fear the wind."
~African Proverb~
(Strong foundations make you unshakable, no matter life's storms.)

32

MORE FROM WOMEN LIKE ME

STORIES THAT HEAL. VOICES THAT RISE. BOOKS THAT MATTER.

At Women Like Me, we believe that every woman carries a story inside her. A story that aches to be heard, a truth that has the power to heal, inspire, and transform. What began as a mission to help women write their truths has now evolved into a global movement, one that has published over 38 books and amplified the voices of more than 180 women from around the world, resulting in over 350 true-life stories being told.

Each book is a thread in the tapestry of this movement.

Each story a sacred offering.

And every author, a woman who chose courage over silence.

Some of these books were born from pain. Others from celebration. All of them carry the fingerprints of resilience, hope, and unshakable spirit.

You'll find stories of survival, motherhood, loss, love, trauma, second chances, sisterhood, and the kind of bold truth-telling that shakes something awake in every reader.

This is more than publishing.

This is legacy work.

This is what happens when women stop apologizing and start writing.

Below, you'll find a list of every title we've released... both from our Women Like Me authors and from my own personal journey.

These are not just books.

They are proof.

Proof that stories can build bridges.

Proof that healing is contagious.

Proof that your voice matters.

Welcome to the Women Like Me library. A living archive of brave hearts and bold truths.

Women Like Me Book Series

This is a collection in which women open their hearts, sharing chapters of their lives to inspire and guide others on their journey through life.

Women Like Me Chapter Series
Where women tell a story of their lives

- A Celebration of Courage and Triumphs
- Stories of Resilience and Courage
- A Tribute to the Brave and Wise
- Breaking Through the Silence
- From Loss to Living

- Healing and Acceptance
- Reclaiming Our Power
- Whispers of Warriors: Women Who Refused to Stay Broken
- Embracing the Unseen – The Courage to Surrender
- Transforming Pain Into Wisdom and Love
- When Life Breaks You Open - Moments That Change Everything
- Beautiful, Broken, Becoming: Real Stories Of Women Growing Through Chaos, Self-Doubt, And Second Chances

---

Women Like Me Community Book Series
These are shorter stories and themed books written by community members.

The community books are a testament to the power of our beautiful members from all around the world. These remarkable women share their thoughts, experiences, and wisdom. Any Women Like Me Community member can write in the community books.

- Messages to My Younger Self
- Sharing Words of Gratitude
- Sharing What We Know to Be True
- Journal for Self-Discovery
- Sharing Life's Important Lessons
- Having Better Relationships
- Honoring the Women in Our Lives
- Letters to Our Future Selves
- The Warrior Within
- Whispers Within the Power of Women's Intuition
- Dreams That Speak the Power Of Women's Dreams

- Graceful Guidance, Treasured Advice, and Love From One Generation to The Next
- Whispers of the Heart: True Stories of Love and Wisdom
- Lessons From Mom
- The Quiet Ones Who Saved Us: Pets That Became Our Lifeline

Women Like Me in Kenya

100% of the profits go directly to these 26 Kenyan Authors. The Women Like Me Book Program covers all costs of producing and publishing the Kenyan books.

These women are mostly widowed and live in extreme poverty. They use the proceeds to pay school fees, allowing their children to receive an education. No school fees mean children cannot go to school. They also purchase food and clothing for their children.

If you would like to support these amazing women in Kenya, please reach out to Julie at julie@changeyourpath.ca

- Strong Women in Kenya
- Through the Eyes of Kenyan Women
- The Children of Kenya
- Kenyan Women Share Their Strength, Wisdom & Love

SALES AND PERSONAL GROWTH

Julie Fairhurst offers a wealth of knowledge through her books on achieving success in business and life. With a remarkable 34-year career as an entrepreneur, her expertise spans sales, marketing, promotion, and writing.

At her website you'll find resources, authors, digital course and more.

www.juliefairhurst.com

- The Julie Fairhurst Story – Healing Generations, One Story at a Time
- From Idea to Bestseller – Writing for Self-Help Authors
- Positivity Makes All the Difference
- Powerful Persuasion – Unlocking the Five Key Strategies for Business Success
- Transferring Enthusiasm - The Sales Book for Your Business Growth
- Agent Matchmaker: How to Find Your Real Estate Soulmate"
- Agent Etiquette – 14 Things You Didn't Learn in Real Estate School
- 7 Keys to Success – How to Become a Real Estate Badass
- 30 Days to Real Estate Action – Real Strategies & Real Connections
- Why Agents Quit the Business

"A river does not flow through the forest
without bringing down trees."
~African Proverb~
(Real change always leaves a mark, progress comes with disruption.)

33

JULIE FAIRHURST

EMPOWERING WOMEN THROUGH STORYTELLING AND INFLUENCE

Julie Fairhurst is the visionary **Founder of the Women Like Me Book Program**, a groundbreaking initiative that has empowered over **160 women to become published authors**. With **300+ true-life stories published** and **over 30 books released**, many of which have achieved **#1 Best Seller status**, Julie has created a platform where women can share their voices, inspire others, and leave a lasting legacy.

What sets the **Women Like Me Book Program** apart is its commitment to accessibility and empowerment. Some women in the program are given the opportunity to **become published authors at no cost**, ensuring that every woman, regardless of financial circumstances, has the chance to share her truth with the world.

Beyond publishing, Julie is a **renowned speaker, trainer, and educator** with **34 years of expertise in sales and marketing**. A **Master Persuader** with deep insights into human behavior, she specializes in helping **women entrepreneurs** build **influence, establish authority, and increase**

revenue through powerful storytelling, strategic marketing, and high-impact sales techniques.

Julie's personal journey, marked by **overcoming adversity, loss, and hardship**, has fueled her passion for **mentoring women**, guiding them to **rise above their challenges, own their stories, and embrace their fullest potential**.

Whether through her books, coaching, or speaking engagements, Julie's mission is clear: **to inspire, uplift, and transform lives —one story at a time.**

Connect with Julie...

- Website – www.juliefairhurst.com
- Email: julie@changeyourpath.ca
- Media Kit – www.juliefairhurst.com

"No matter how full the river, it still wants to grow."
~Congolese Proverb~
(There is always room to grow, learn, and become more; never stop
flowing forward.)

www.ingramcontent.com/pod-product-compliance
Lightning Source LLC
LaVergne TN
LVHW051122080426
835510LV00018B/2191